Old Pitlochry, Strathtummel an

by Bernard Byrom

C000083200

A photograph taken in Edwardian days at the junction of Pitlochry's Station Road (on the right) and Main Street (now Atholl Road), with Birnam Place running off to the left just before the Craigower Hotel. An elegant lady is being driven down the street by a coachman in a coach-and-pair but the writing was already on the wall for this form of transport - notice the early motor car parked on the opposite side of the street in front of the creeper-covered buildings. Reid's Temperance Hotel on the left was owned by an architect, John Reid, but run by Mrs Jessie Reid (probably his wife). The Craigower Hotel was also a Temperance establishment, run by Mrs Christina Hunter. The hotel occupied most of the upper floor of this building but the shops on the arcaded ground floor were occupied by P.K. Donald (painter), Robert Stewart (stationer), Peter Gould (jeweller, tobacconist and hairdresser), George Stöbie (fruiterer), and Henry & Charles Frazer (clothiers). The shop on the corner of Station Road belonged to W. Miller (grocer). On the other side of the road Reid's Hotel is now McKay's Hotel and the Craigower Hotel is now the Pitlochry Backpackers' Hotel. The ground-floor shops are currently Brats Children's Clothing, Mackintosh Jewellery and Gifts, Hawkshead Clothing, Perthshire Woollens, Lloyds Pharmacy and Pitlochry Knitwear.

Text © Bernard Byrom, 2006.
First published in the United Kingdom, 2006,
by Stenlake Publishing Ltd.
54–58 Mill Square
Catrine
KA5 6RD
www.stenlake.co.uk

ISBN 9781840333718

A similar view to the previous picture but taken around 30 or 40 years later. The appearance of the buildings has hardly changed but the type of traffic certainly has. Reid's Hotel has now become McKay's Hotel and an electric light has replaced the gas lamp on the pavement in front of it. Next door the Craigower Hotel is proudly advertising hot and cold water in every bedroom, whilst further down the street, on the end of Alba Place, is a sign advertising the Pitlochry Motor Company's garage. The shops under the Craigower Hotel are Robert H. Stewart (stationer), Peter Gould (jeweller and watchmaker), Norwells Footwear, and Frazer & Sons (clothiers).

Further Reading

The books listed below were used by the author during his research. None of them is available from Stenlake Publishing. Those interested in finding out more are advised to contact their local bookshop or reference library.

John H. Dixon, *Pitlochry Past and Present*, 1925.
Jeremy Duncan, *Perth & Kinross - The Big County*, 1997.
Seton Gordon, *Highways and Byways in the Central Highlands*, 1995.
Nick Haynes, *Perth & Kinross: an illustrated architectural guide*, 2000.
Colin Liddell, *Pitlochry - Heritage of a Highland District*, 1993.
Archie McKerracher, *Perthshire in History and Legend*, 1988, revised 2000.
North Perthshire Family History Group, *Moulin Church Memorial Inscriptions*, 2005.
Leslie's Directories, 1897–1940.
Queen Victoria's *Scottish Diaries*.
The Statistical Accounts of Scotland, 1791–1799.
The New Statistical Account of Scotland, 1845.
Valuation Rolls of the County of Perth, 1855 onwards.

Acknowledgements

The author wishes to thank the following for their help: Glenda and Linda, Pitlochry Visitor Information Centre; Atholl Palace Hotel, Pitlochry; the Hydro Hotel, Pitlochry. Special thanks are due to Sandy Wilson of Pitlochry for the invaluable help he gave in checking and occasionally correcting captions and for sharing his encyclopaedic knowledge of the area.

INTRODUCTION

Pitlochry as we know it today is basically a Victorian creation, although it owes its existence in the first place to General Wade who, in 1727, built his military road along the valley between Dunkeld and Killicrankie. Until that time the main road to the north had followed the higher ground on the north side of the valley and passed through the village of Moulin where it crossed the road which ran from Strathtay, via the ferry at Port-na-Craig, to Strathardle.

Moulin was an ancient Pictish settlement which, because of its strategic importance, used to be protected by a double ring of forts. It also became an important ecclesiastical centre; its first church was founded around the fifth century AD by St Colm, an Irish Pict who came to Scotland with St Fillan. In 1180 Malcolm, Earl of Atholl, granted the church and its lands to the Abbey of Dunfermline in return for their monks saying daily masses for the souls of his wife and himself. He obviously regarded this as an insurance policy, which would enable him and his wife to enjoy eternal life in heaven after their deaths.

For centuries Pitlochry comprised three small hamlets at the bottom of the valley and situated on both sides of the Moulin Burn. They did not acquire that name until much later and Moulin was the main settlement in the area. However, when General Wade was sent by the government to build a network of main roads throughout the Highlands following the first Jacobite rebellion (so that government troops could be quickly deployed to quell any future uprisings), he built one along the bottom of the valley, through the hamlets, and subsequently the centre of importance moved from Moulin to them.

The second great influence on Pitlochry's development was Queen Victoria's love of the Highlands. She first came to the area with Prince Albert in 1842, visiting Dunkeld and Taymouth Castle, and she returned again in 1844, renting Blair Castle for three weeks and touring the area on horseback and by private carriage. She paid further visits to the Pitlochry area in 1861, 1865 and 1866, while staying at Balmoral.

Apart from the Queen's personal liking for the area, which made it fashionable with others, Pitlochry also had the personal approval of her physician, Sir James Clark, who declared its spa waters to be remedial and recommended his wealthy London patients to spend their holidays there. Hydropathic establishments, where patients received treatment of hot and cold baths, were popular at the time and two magnificent ones were built in the town when this style of treatment went out of fashion these were converted into conventional luxury hotels.

The third great influence on creating the Pitlochry of today was the arrival of the railway from the south in 1863, which brought a great influx of visitors to the town and encouraged the building of shops, villas and hotels to cater for them. Wealthy tourists and sportsmen would rent villas for weeks on end, bringing with them a retinue of domestic servants whilst, at the other end of the scale, hundreds of manufacturing workers would descend on the town from dozens of excursion trains run on bank holidays from Edinburgh, Glasgow and Dundee.

In the early nineteenth century Pitlochry had seven licensed distilleries and a brewery, as well as a meal mill that had been relocated from a site near the Tummel up to a higher level its former mill pond became the garden of Fisher's Hotel; the mill closed down in 1923 and is now the Old Mill Restaurant. The distilleries produced an average of 90,000 gallons of whisky per year and most went to outlets in Dundee but some went to Edinburgh, Glasgow and London. Only one of these distilleries remains today, located at Aldour at the east end of the town and producing the 'Blair Athol' single malt whisky. The brewery was never much of a commercial success and was closed around 1870.

Gas was introduced into the village as early as 1830 when Messrs Conacher erected a small gas works in connection with their house and shop which were subsequently incorporated into Scotland's Hotel. However, it didn't become widely available in the village until the 1890s and electricity didn't arrive until 1930; some houses weren't connected until after the Second World War.

Pitlochry, which achieved burgh status in 1947, has continued to thrive and prosper. Probably its major physical change has been caused by the post-war hydroelectric scheme which created the man-made Loch Faskally on its doorstep. Its dam on the River Tummel and its 'ladder', which enables salmon to reach their traditional spawning grounds upstream, have become tourist attractions in their own right, as has the Festival Theatre which began on a small-scale in 1951 and has since achieved international recognition.

A few miles north of the town towards the Pass of Killiecrankie, the B8019 leaves the A9 trunk road, crosses the River Garry and strikes westwards towards Loch Tummel. This is the traditional 'Road to the Isles' as immortalised in the chorus of the song written in 1917 by Kenneth MacLeod, with music by Marjory Kennedy-Fraser, as a marching song for the Highland regiments during the darkest days of the First World War - 'Sure, by Tummel and Loch Rannoch and Lochaber I will go/By heather tracks wi' heaven in their wiles.'

Most people nowadays think of the road to the isles as being the route taken by the modern A82 road through Glencoe via Fort William to Mallaig but this is not the historical route. This ran westwards from the vicinity of the railway station at Rannoch over boggy tracks across Rannoch Moor towards Fort William and Lochaber. It was the coming of decent coach roads, coupled to the inability to drain Rannoch Moor in the vicinity of the tracks, that led to their replacement by the present route.

Loch Tummel is around 6 miles long, ending at Tummel Bridge at which General Wade's hump-backed bridge of 1730 is situated alongside a modern road bridge. This is a popular spot for tourists; there is a holiday village here and a new Loch Tummel Hotel owned by Lochs and Glens Holidays.

Continuing westwards the road passes through the historic Dunalastair estate, seat of the Robertsons of Struan. At the eastern end of Loch Rannoch is the lovely village of Kinloch Rannoch, which was originally settled by government soldiers sent to the area to suppress the Highland clans in the aftermath of the 1745 Jacobite rebellion. The minister of the parish, writing in the *Statistical Account of Scotland* in 1793, painted a grim picture of living conditions in the area a few years earlier: 'Around the above period [1754] the bulk of the tenants in Rannoch had no such things as beds. They lay on the ground, with a little heather or fern under them. One single blanket was all their bedclothes, excepting their body clothes. Now they have standing-up beds and abundance of blankets. At that time the houses in Rannoch were what they called "Stake and Rife". One could not enter except on all fours and, after entering, it was impossible to stand upright. Now there are comfortable houses built of stone.'

This used to be a particularly lawless area in which blackmail was extensively practiced. The same minister wrote, 'They [the blackmailers] laid the whole country, from Stirling to Coupar of Angus, under contribution, obliging the inhabitants to pay them Black Mail, as it is called, to save their property from being plundered. This was the centre of this kind of traffic. In the months of September and October they gathered to the number of about 300, built temporary huts, drank whisky all the time, settled accounts for stolen cattle and received balances. Every man then bore arms. It would have required a regiment to have brought a thief from that country.'

Both the Strathtummel and Rannoch areas suffered during the Highland Clearances when small crofters were driven out of their ancestral homes by their landlords who replaced them by more profitable sheep farms. Some of the displaced families moved south to find employment in the manufacturing districts of the Forth-Clyde belt or the textile industries of northern England, but many emigrated to North America or the colonies.

Continuing still further westwards the road passes Loch Rannoch, 12 miles long, and the scenery becomes increasingly wild and desolate until Rannoch Station on the West Highland Railway is reached. This is near the summit of the bleak Rannoch Moor, where the ground is dotted with peaty, boggy pools and the roots of trees from the prehistoric Caledonian Forest - which once covered these parts - protrude eerily from the soil. This is not only the end of this book's journey from Pitlochry, it is the end of the road itself.

Another early view again looking eastwards down the main street. The creeper-covered building on the left was a private house and next to it was the shop of James Duncan (shoemaker), who subsequently relocated a few yards down the street to the new shops in Alba Place. The house later became tearooms and Duncan's shop became Stewart's Bakery (the site of this shop is nowadays the premises of Pitlochry Knitwear). Beyond them, on the other side of West Moulin Road, the shop with the veranda belonged to William Robertson (chemist). Davidson's Chemists shop now occupies the nearer half of the building and James Pringle (knitwear) occupy the further part. The block beyond is Alba Place, built in 1897 and described in more detail later in this book. On the opposite side of the road the nearest shop is Charles C. Stuart & Son who were licensed grocers and seedsmen as well as being agents for P. & P. Campbell, the dyers. Next to it was the large shop owned by Mitchell Brothers who sold a range of woollen goods as well as being dressmakers and milliners. These shops are now the premises of The Golf Company and W.H. Smith respectively; the furthest shop is now Keep Sakes Gift Shop.

The new post office was the centrepiece of this imposing building, erected in 1897 and named Alba Place. It was built by Alex Robertson at a cost of more than £5,000 and has a 130-foot frontage, the ground floor being business premises and the upper floor containing flats. Pitlochry's first post office opened sometime between 1811 and 1821; this new building was its third home. Its accommodation comprised a public office, telegraph room, sorting room, and waiting room. Alba Place's business occupants in this picture were Wm. Brown & Co. (grocers and butchers), the post office, Lachlan McKay (stationer), James Duncan & Son (shoemakers), and Miss Margaret Robertson (fancy goods). The latter three businesses were original tenants of the block. At the far end, advertised by a prominent sign but out of sight round the corner, was Russell's Garage. The same premises are nowadays occupied by the Royal Bank of Scotland, For the Present gift shop, the post office, House of Scotland gift shop, Haddows wine merchants, and Heritage Jewellers. Russells Garage is no more; its building is now part of James Pringle (knitwear).

This 1926 view of the main street is looking westwards with Fisher's Hotel on the left and Alba Place on the right. Behind the group of people in the foreground is the Butter Memorial Fountain, built in 1887 of Aberdeen granite in the shape of a gothic spire. It was erected in memory of the late Lieutenant-colonel Archibald Butter the younger of Faskally who had died in 1880, aged 44. The memorial was located in the space between the Royal Bank and the Bank of Scotland. Large concert parties were held beside it in summer in the days before the First World War. By the mid-1960s it was felt to be in the way of modern traffic and needed to be relocated to another part of the town. Accordingly, it was dismantled in 1965 and its stones were individually numbered. Unfortunately, by the time funds were available for its re-erection, all the stones had disappeared and only the memorial plaque could be found; this is now displayed in a small memorial garden built adjacent to the site of the fountain.

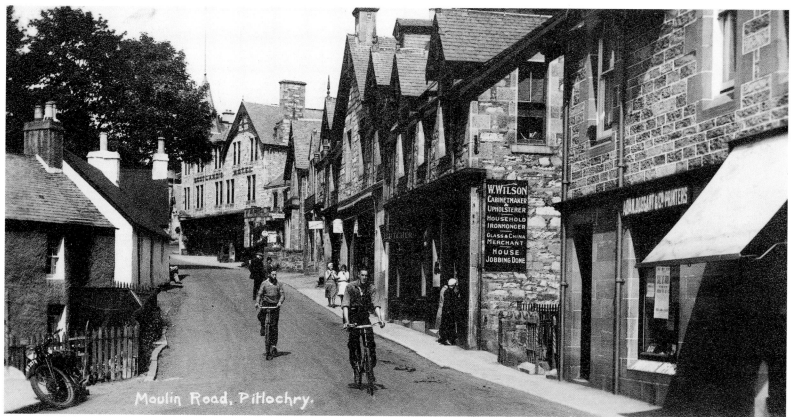

Moulin Road, Pitlochry.

This road, which runs north from the main street past Scotland's Hotel has undergone a number of name changes over the years. It was originally called West Moulin Road and then, after the present-day West Moulin Road was built, it was renamed Mid Moulin Road. Finally, it received its present name of Bonnethill Road to commemorate a colony of bonnet makers from Glasgow who came to the village in the nineteenth century and occupied two thatched cottages on the west side of the road just beyond where the Lloyds TSB bank stands today. Here they manufactured a distinctive type of male headgear that became known as the Pitlochry Bonnet. This was a circular hat with a band above the forehead; its felted material then tapered upwards and was topped with a bobble in a similar style to a Balmoral bonnet. The view up the right-hand side of the road is little changed today. The shop on the extreme right is now Ian Kemp Electrical but it still has the 'Adam Doggart & Co.' sign visible here. Next door is 'That Barber', followed by an alleyway. The next building is still a butcher's shop, nowadays occupied by Macdonald Bros., followed by Stevens of Pitlochry Furniture, and Mor' Anda Hair and Beauty. In the next building, beyond the pathway, are Walton Kilgour (chartered accountants) and the British Red Cross shop. Then comes a private house and, finally, Scotland's Hotel. The buildings on the left side of the road have changed more drastically. The building at the junction with Atholl Road is currently a ladies' outfitters, then comes the Moulin Burn and beyond it, standing in front of the site of the Atholl Aerated Waterworks (better known as Martin's lemonade factory), there is now the Lloyds TSB building.

This is the oldest hostelry in Pitlochry and was originally called the Star Inn. Messrs Connacher introduced gas lighting - then a novelty - to it in 1830. The hotel was bought in 1880 by John Scotland who redeveloped and extended it on all sides, as well as renaming it after himself; nowadays it has 72 rooms. It was managed by his daughters, Nellie and Eva Scotland. The exterior of the hotel in this Victorian view is instantly recognisable today. The castellated bow window, which was a feature of the old Star Inn over 150 years ago, is still there; the only casualty appears to have been the adjacent premises in the picture of J. & P. McLauchlan (butchers and poulterers), whose shop has been completely demolished except for its back wall. The shop on the left, which belonged to Hugh MacDonald (tailor), is nowadays a private house, but the portion jutting out into the road is still a shop, the Video Shack. The turreted building beyond Scotland's Hotel is nowadays part of that hotel's accommodation but originally housed the Bank of Scotland. At the top of the hill, in the background, is the Pitlochry Hydro.

PITLOCHRY, WEST.   F.H.

These spacious cottages on the main road at the west end of the town used to be the premises of the Perth Banking Company which was established in the village in 1853. It was taken over in 1858 by the Union Bank and moved to new premises further east (where the council offices now are), but these buildings are still known as the Old Bank Buildings. This picture appears to have been taken at the height of an Edwardian summer's day; a water cart is being driven towards the village centre, the pipe at the rear spraying the unmetalled road in an effort to keep down the clouds of dust that inevitably rose up on such days. The cottages are nowadays numbered 148 (self-catering apartments), 150 (Lamb House) and 152 Atholl Road. Beyond them, the white building housed the smithy which closed in the mid-1960s; it is now the Old Smithy restaurant and tea rooms.

In this view, looking eastwards from Strathview Terrace, the house in the left foreground is named 'Dalhouzie' and the long building behind it is Macnaughton's factory and warehouse. Although it cannot be seen in the photograph, West Moulin Road runs between these two buildings. Macnaughton had extensive water-powered mills here which were established in 1835 and manufactured tweed cloth from raw wool. The buildings in the foreground had wooden walls with a slated roof. The mills closed for production in 1980 and subsequently suffered a major fire in which the wooden buildings were destroyed. The stone buildings of the mill survived the fire and in 1988 were converted into Penny's supermarket which subsequently became today's Co-op supermarket. Its car park occupies the site of the wooden buildings. The church on the left of the picture is known locally as 'Mount Zion Church'. It was built in 1884 as the West Church to serve the town and summer visitors because the heritors refused to relocate the parish church from Moulin, but twentieth century changes have resulted in Moulin church being closed and 'Mount Zion' is now the parish church. Beyond it can be seen the roof and tower of the former East Church, nowadays converted into flats.

This famous posting hotel was built in the middle of the village around 1839 and was owned around the mid-nineteenth century by Donald Fisher who gave his name to it. There were stables to the rear, tennis courts, and gardens which were created on the site of the mill dam after the old mill was relocated to the side of the Moulin Burn. The gardens were extensive and, in their heyday, were one of the sights of the Highlands. They used to be visible from the main road and local legend has it that when Mr Robertson built Alba Place opposite the hotel and cut out Mr Fisher's view of Ben-y-Vrackie, Mr Fisher retaliated by building the wing of the hotel on the left of the picture with the remark, 'If he won't let me see Ben-y-Vrackie, I won't let him see my gardens!' This new wing was at least built in sympathy with the architecture of the main buildings. In more recent years another wing has been built parallel to it, joining the main building at the junction of the taller and smaller sections. This not only cuts out the spacious view shown in the picture but, being built in a more modern style, is not as much in keeping architecturally with the rest of the hotel. Luckily, the interior of the hotel itself still offers good Scottish hospitality to the traveller.

This hotel was designed by Andrew Heiton Jnr and opened in 1878 as the Athole Hydropathic. It was built in the style of a French chateau with great circular towers and large pavilion-roofed wings; the public rooms are characterised by enormous scale and theatrical opulence. Its cost of nearly £100,000 almost bankrupted its owners; as early as 1886 it went into liquidation and was bought by William Macdonald for only £25,000! Macdonald soon realised that more money could be made from offering entertainment to guests rather than medical cures and so he transformed the hotel into a luxurious conventional hotel. Unfortunately, he became involved in an unconnected business venture which turned out disastrously for him and in 1909 he was made bankrupt, the hotel being seized as part of his assets. In 1913 it was purchased by members of the Public Schools Alpine Sports Club Ltd who renamed it the Atholl Palace Hotel. Since then it has changed ownership several times, its latest owners being a consortium of Dublin businessmen who purchased it in 2001. During the First World War the hotel was used as a school for the pupils of Queen Margaret's School, Scarborough, who had been forced to leave their school after it was badly damaged when Scarborough was shelled in 1915 by a German cruiser; they remained at the hotel for the rest of the war. During the Second World War the hotel was used as a school for evacuated children by the pupils of St Joseph's R.C. School in Glasgow and Leys School, Cambridge. For many years the hotel was only open for five months of the year, from around the end of May until the beginning of October, but nowadays it is an all-season venue for holidays and conferences. A museum illustrating the history and development of the hotel from its opening up to the present day has been created on the garden level where visitors' servants used to be accommodated and the resident doctor used to administer hydropathic treatment to guests.

The Atholl Palace has extensive grounds and has always excelled in sporting facilities, including its own golf course and shooting range. From its earliest days it had three tennis courts and in 1924 a further four courts were added. The Highland Lawn Tennis Championships were established in 1896 and are still played there.

Edwardian elegance on a grand scale - a corner of the spacious Drawing Room at the Atholl Palace. This room later became the ballroom and was the venue for weekly tea dances. It is nowadays called the Bow Lounge and is used for larger functions such as wedding receptions. The sprung strip wood dance floor and the large picture windows are original features and the two fireplaces are still intact, but the solid wood doors at the far end of the room and the ceiling roses have been replaced.

"The Dashing White Sergeant"

ATHOLL PALACE HOTEL
PITLOCHRY

HIGHLAND OCCASIONS
1935

PROGRAMME

MAY · JUNE
JULY

AUGUST
SEPTEMBER

1935			1935		
May	16th	Hotel Opens. First Footing.	Aug.	2nd	Highland Tattoo.
„	18th	Opening Competition on re-constructed Golf Course.	„	16th	Grouse Ball (Fancy Dress).
June	5th	Derby Night Dinner Dance.	„	19-23rd	Highland Open Amateur Golf Championship.
„	7th	Evening Cruise on Loch Tay.	„	24th	Sheep Dog Trials.
„	10th	Highland Tattoo.	„	30th	"Harvest Home" Carnival Dance.
„	21st	Midsummer Revels and Carnival Dance.	Sept.	7th	Pitlochry Highland Games.
„	28th	The Palace Pierrots of 1935.	„	9-14th	Championship of the Highlands Lawn Tennis Tournament.
July	2-4th	Ladies' Golf Tournament—Atholl Cup.	„	13th	Tennis Ball.
„	5th	Highland Tattoo.	„	20th	Highland Tattoo.
„	12th	Evening Cruise on Loch Tay.	„	27th	Autumn Ball.
„	19th	Carnival Dance.			
„	26th	Soft Lights and Sweet Music.			

NOTE. — THIS PROGRAMME IS SUBJECT TO ALTERATION.

Throughout the season, Lawn Tennis Tournaments, Putting and Golf Competitions will be arranged weekly. Particulars will be given on the Hotel Notice Board. Dancing takes place every evening except Sunday.

THE DASHING WHITE SERGEANT SAYS—

They've asked me to say something about the doings up at my billet this year, an' after a dekko at the programme, it seems to me that it's better than ever—You know, tattoos, evenin' cruises an' all kinds o' carnival do's. Don't know 'ow they have the face to put that pier-rot show on again, though it was funny in parts they didn't mean to be.

Then there's the 'Arvest 'Ome when everybody's got to dress up in something country-like—bew-colic the bloke calls it. I 'ope it don't give 'em the colic! They're givin' prizes for the best dairy maids an' shepherdesses and ploughmen an' village idiots an' so on. I 'opes they don't give the village idiot prize to some bloke wots not playin'

I might say a lot more about it but I've got my stripes to think of.

This programme of 'Highland Occasions' from the Atholl Palace's 1935 season give an idea of what well-to-do visitors to the hotel could expect for entertainment. Note that guests could enjoy dancing in the hotel ballroom every night of the week except Sundays.

A 4-6-0 locomotive, No. 14690 'Dalcross Castle', built for the Highland Railway in 1913 by the North British Locomotive Company and originally numbered 43, calls at Pitlochry with a southbound stopping train to Perth in London Midland & Scottish days. The line opened to Pitlochry from Dunkeld on 1 June 1863 and from Inverness via Forres and Aviemore on 9 September in the same year. The owning company was the Inverness & Perth Junction Railway which absorbed the Perth & Dunkeld Railway in the following year to become the Highland Railway. Eventually the Highland Railway extended all the way from Perth to Wick and Thurso; its principal branch is the 82-mile line from Dingwall to Kyle of Lochalsh. At the 1923 'Grouping' of Britain's railways into four large companies, the Highland Railway became part of the London Midland & Scottish Railway (LMS); nationalisation in 1948 brought it into the Scottish Region of British Railways and, with privatisation, the line is now operated by First Scotrail. Unusually for a main line, it is predominantly single-track with crossing loops at the principal stations.

Pitlochry Station.

Returning Edwardian holidaymakers throng the southbound platform at Pitlochry Station as they await their train home. In spite of their numbers the amount of luggage on the platform is quite small because it was the practice for holidaymakers to send their heavy luggage in advance, collected from their doorstep and delivered direct to their hotel and vice versa. The first Pitlochry Station was built in 1863, but was rebuilt (as shown in this picture) around 1890 in an H-plan layout with a canopy infilling the space between the wings on the platform side. The crowstepped gables, tall chimneys and decorative ridging are in typical Highland Railway style. Only six days after the line opened Queen Victoria travelled along it in a special train from Perth to Blair Atholl. It was a sad occasion for her; she had interrupted her journey from Windsor to Balmoral especially to visit her old friend, the sixth Duke of Atholl, who was terminally ill at his home at Blair Castle. In spite of his condition the Duke insisted on rising from his bed and dressing and he even managed to escort the Queen back to her special train at the station; from there she travelled back to rejoin the Royal Train at Stanley Junction and continued her journey to Balmoral. It was their last meeting, as the Duke died only four months later.

The Cuilc is a large pond situated just below Pitlochry Golf Club and its name derives from the Gaelic word for sedges or reeds. The area was formerly marshland and farmers used to dig deeply in it for marl which is soil containing carbonate of lime and highly regarded as a fertiliser. The pond used to be much larger and discharged to the west, but in the fifteenth century a deep cutting was made to divert it eastwards to supplement the water supply for the meal mill in Pitlochry. At a later date water was supplied via a pipe to the railway station to replenish the water supplies of steam locomotives about to begin their northbound climb over the summits of Drummochter and Slochd McHuic. In the course of digging in the 1770s farmers dug up the skulls of four giant oxen. They were identified as being uri (Bos primigenius) that had roamed the country in Neolithic times.

The first Pitlochry golf course was constructed early in the twentieth century as a 9-hole course on the banks of the River Tummel. The holes weaved their way down from near the Green Park Hotel to the pavilion at the recreation ground and back again. Members soon became ambitious to have a larger course and Colonel Charles Butter of Cluniemore, who was a major landowner in the area, leased the necessary amount of land at Drumchory Farm to Pitlochry Golf Club Ltd. The course was constructed during 1908 by Willie Fernie of Troon and its initial layout was quite different to today's; it included two par 5 holes and the eighteenth hole incorporated the present-day seventeenth and eighteenth. In the early 1920s Major Cecil Hutchison tinkered and tweaked it to produce the present-day course. The initial length was 5,695 yards, but this has been increased over the years to 5,811 yards, par 69 for men and just over 5,200 yards for ladies with a par of 72. The clubhouse, situated a little above the east corner of the Cuilc, was opened in 1909 with a big ceremony. Its exterior appearance is just the same today but the eighteenth green has changed somewhat and the hole is now over to the left of the picture. The old course is now submerged beneath the waters of Loch Faskally.

The first public school in Pitlochry was located at the eastern end of the town on the north side of Atholl Road and was opened in 1873 to replace two existing schools. Expansion of the village resulted in this school soon becoming too small for local needs and a new school, pictured here, was built in East Moulin Road at a cost of around £5,000. It was a single-storied building in the Gothic style, designed by C.S. Robertson of Perth, and was regarded as the best of 32 designs submitted. The school was opened on 2 May 1898 as a combined school for Pitlochry and Moulin. After 1935 it was known as Pitlochry High School but senior pupils were sent to Aberfeldy for their fifth and sixth year studies after 1960. Unfortunately the school burned down in January 1974. It was replaced the following year by the present-day school, which is situated just to the north of the old school, but its ruins were not removed until 1990.

Edwardian holidaymakers pose for a photograph outside the Pitlochry Hydro Hotel. The coach-and-pair, driven by a liveried coachman, is well patronised - maybe they were off for a tour of the area. The hotel used to have a garage, tennis courts and golf course. The tennis courts are now part of the car park and the golf course lies under new housing, but the hotel does have a putting green and a croquet lawn nowadays. The hotel was originally owned by Mr James Sorley Robertson and was a Temperance Hotel until Scottish Highlands Hotels bought it in 1930. In earlier years it was only open from Easter to the beginning of October. Since 1998 the hotel has been owned by Shearings who have turned it into a popular all-year-round venue and touring base for their Scottish touring holidays.

In this picture the front entrance of the Hydro is on the right-hand side, which faces south. The hotel was built in two stages: the first stage was the western part in 1890, with 30 bedrooms, and the second stage in 1900 added another 40. As was customary in those days, relatively few of these rooms had private facilities and many internal alterations have been made over the years to provide them all with en-suite facilities. In 1989 a leisure centre was built onto the west front of the hotel, which has rather spoiled the aesthetic appearance of that side of the building. Fortunately, the view of it from the road is nowadays totally obscured by the trees on the left which have matured and grown to an enormous height. The house on the right of the picture is 'Dun–Donnachaidh'. The Bowling Club was formed in 1887 and played on the green situated between Bonnethill Road and West Moulin Road. The first pavilion was a picturesque structure with a thatched roof, which accidentally burned down after an attempt to smoke out a beehive. The second pavilion is the one in the picture, but was inadequate for the job, and the present one was opened in May 1933. It was designed by a local man, John Brander, and has since been considerably altered and extended.

This pool on West Moulin Road was built in 1933 by unemployed ex-servicemen. It was intended to be a children's sailing pond and, at the opening ceremony, Mrs Butter launched a toy yacht. It later became a paddling pool but fell into disuse and was closed many years ago.

This house, No. 11 Toberargan Road, is known as the Wellhouse. Toberargan was the name of one of the three hamlets that combined in the eighteenth century to make up Pitlochry and it contains the well of St Feargain, which is translated in English as Toberargan. A century ago it was a shop owned by a grocer named William Robert Longmire, but for many years past it has been a bed and breakfast establishment still named 'The Wellhouse'. Standing as it does on the corner of the street, the veranda in the picture was forever being damaged by lorries turning the corner and was eventually taken down. The present-day railings at the front of the house are modern replacements in a similar style to those pictured but the George V postbox remains intact. The bricked-up doorway on the right used to be the entrance to the shop.

This fine house, which is situated off West Moulin Road, was built for Robertson the joiner and is nowadays the Craig Mhor Guest House. Rectangular modern extensions have been built onto its southern and western sides, which spoil its gracious lines, but otherwise the exterior of the house appears unchanged. It no longer has the spacious grounds that surround it in the picture; nowadays it is surrounded by the modern housing of Lettoch Terrace and Lettoch Place. The pond in the bottom right corner is the old mill pond which was formed by damming the Moulin Burn at this point to provide an enhanced supply of water downstream to both the Pitlochry meal mill and Macnaughton's tweed mills.

The original Bonskeid House, sited in terraced gardens and woodland near the Queen's View at the eastern end of Loch Tummel, was built in the classical style in 1796 on land belonging to Dr and Mrs Stewart of Fincastle. Their daughter married George Freeland Barbour whose family had made their fortune in the Manchester cotton trade and in 1869 the couple had the building extensively extended and remodelled in the fashionable Scottish Baronial style. The house was remodelled for them by Andrew Heiton Jnr in 1881 into the baronial tower house pictured here and was further remodelled in 1909 and in the 1970s. In 1921 the then owner, Freeland Barbour, who was a deeply religious man and keenly interested in the work of the YMCA, offered it to them as tenants. They remained as tenants until 1951 when they bought it outright. In 1960 they added a large dining room but, although the accommodation was extensively renovated in the 1990s, it was still Spartan in places and some of the larger rooms in the old building were furnished in a dormitory style, which suited younger members better than others. Having run the house as a Christian conference and retreat centre since 1921, harsh economics forced the YMCA to sell the property at the end of the twentieth century and the house is once again privately owned.

Old Fincastle House, which is located high on the north side of Loch Tummel, was a seventeenth century seat of a branch of the Stewarts who were heavily involved in the 1745 Jacobite uprisings. There was once a church about 600 yards away from the house but it fell into ruin in the 1700s. No trace now remains of this church and it is believed that its stones and the tombstones in its adjoining graveyard were used to build an extension to the house. Certainly the lintel over the main doorway is an old tombstone from the churchyard. There are inscriptions on the walls which tell the history of the house and of the Stewart family who lived in it. The Barbour family are their descendants by marriage and still live in the area.

Above: The ferry across the River Tummel at Port-na-Craig was established in the twelfth century by the monks of Coupar Angus who had been gifted the lands of Fonab. The ferry conveyed horses and carts as well as foot passengers. The building on the far side of the river is the Ferryman's Inn, which still performs the same functions for travellers today. The last ferryman was Duncan Forbes, who was also the sanitary inspector for the Highland District.

Right: This bouncy public footbridge is constructed of lattice-girder pylons, wire rope cables and rod suspenders, and has a lattice truss span with a wooden deck. It replaced the ferry that had operated at this point since the twelfth century. The bridge was manufactured by the Lanarkshire Steel Company Ltd at a cost of £850 and was funded by public subscription with a grant of £250 from the Highland District Committee. It was erected in memory of Lt–Col. George Glas Sandeman of Fonab and was opened by the local Unionist MP, the Marchioness of Tullibardine, on Empire Day 1913.

The Pitlochry Festival Theatre was the inspiration of the late John Stewart and opened on 19 May 1951 at Lower Oakfield, Pitlochry, in a tent within a tent. The auditorium was in the smaller tent and the stage, dressing rooms and everything else were squeezed into the other one. A storm in August 1952 almost brought disaster when the outer tent was ripped right to the top of its kingpost. The theatre lost £17,000 in its first two years of operation but things began to improve in the following year and it has never looked back since. The tents were replaced in 1953 by a semi-permanent building on the same site which popular demand soon rendered inadequate. This has now become the curling rink and the foundation stone of the present theatre was laid at Port-na-Craig in September 1979, the first performance being given on 19 May 1981. The theatre originally operated only during the summer season but is nowadays open all the year round.

In the years immediately following the Second World War the North of Scotland Hydro-Electric Board undertook a major project to harness the waters of Lochs Eigheach, Garry, Ericht, Rannoch and Tummel to create a huge electricity-generating capacity. The foundation stone of the Faskally Dam was laid by the Countess of Airlie on 25 April 1946; the dam was opened in 1951 and is 145 metres long. The loch thereby created, Faskally (named after the mansion and estate near the head of the loch), is entirely man-made and was created by the waters of the Tummel and the Garry flooding the valley to the north of Pitlochry. In doing so it submerged the Pitlochry recreation ground and the former golf course. This picture shows a view of the dam from upstream on Loch Faskally. Beyond it the water falls into the resumption of the River Tummel, passes the Festival Theatre and flows under the Port-na-Craig suspension bridge on its way past Pitlochry. Because the banks of the river are glacial moraines it was necessary to build huge retaining walls of concrete and stone on both sides of the loch. The biggest of these is on the north side where its length is 275 metres long and no less than 60 metres deep; truly an 'iceberg' situation where the visible part is only a small proportion of the total works.

Salmon and sea trout migrate upstream in spring, summer and early autumn before spawning in the late autumn. The rivers upstream of Pitlochry, such as the Tummel, the Garry and their tributaries, are their destinations. The fish ladder is 310 metres long and comprises a series of 34 pools connected by underwater pipes. Each pool is 50 centimetres higher than the last and a counter records the number of fish that migrate through the pass. The salmon don't actually jump up the ladder but swim through interconnecting pipes. An observation chamber allows visitors to watch the salmon underwater through a large plate glass window.

The creation of Loch Faskally in 1951 not only resulted in the A9 trunk road being diverted to the west of Pitlochry but also caused the demolition of the old Cluny Bridge of 1834 across the Tummel to the north of the town; it was replaced by the present-day Aldour Bridge further down the river. This footbridge was said to be the first bridge in Britain to be built of aluminium-alloy and gives pedestrians access from the old road on the north side of the loch to the footpaths on the south side leading back to the dam, the fish ladder and the Port-na-Craig Suspension Bridge. Adjacent to it, at a higher level, traffic on the new A9 trunk road now thunders across the loch on a concrete viaduct.

The Coronation Bridge crosses the River Tummel about 800 yards upstream of the Falls of Tummel where it takes a sharp turn westwards as it joins the River Garry. It was dedicated on 22 November 1911, which was King George V and Queen Mary's coronation day. Sixty-seven years earlier Queen Victoria had visited the Falls on 17 September 1844 and her visit is commemorated with a small obelisk at the spot. Walkers can cross the bridge and pass the Falls to reach Garry Bridge in the Pass of Killicrankie. An early form of salmon ladder was constructed nearby in 1910 on the north side of the Falls of Tummel to help salmon to clear the falls.

The Vale of Atholl Pipe Band was formed on 3 October 1906 under the presidency of Mr J.M. Dixon. In this picture Pipe Major Mitchell Pirnie is standing on the extreme right of the picture. The band didn't begin to enter competitions until 1976, but by 1979 they had become champions in Grade 3 and are nowadays competing in Grade 1. A Juvenile Band was formed in 1980 and a Novice Juvenile Band in 1991. The band wore the Murray of Atholl tartan until 1993 but then switched to the muted Macnaughton tartan in recognition of their sponsors, A. & J. Macnaughton of Pitlochry.

A group of happy Dundonians enjoying their summer holidays at Pitlochry in August 1905. Everyone is having fun; they are all dressed up in borrowed clothes and some are sporting false whiskers. Pitlochry was a favourite destination of the inhabitants of Dundee, both for days out and for longer holidays. The advent of paid holidays enabled families to spend a whole week away from the smoke and grime of the city, whilst it was usual on bank holidays for several excursion trains to bring in hundreds of day trippers from the Dundee, Glasgow and Edinburgh areas. The only person named in the picture is a Mr Fenton of Dundee who is on the extreme right, wearing a straw hat and holding a sweeping brush.

The hotel in the centre of Moulin village was built in 1695 on what was then the main road from Dunkeld to the north. Today, the exterior appearance of the hotel is very little changed from the time of this picture when young Edwardian lassies were able to stand around in the middle of the village square in complete safety. An additional wing was built onto the left-hand side of the hotel in the twentieth century but happily its architectural style is so much in keeping with the rest of the building that it looks as though it has been there for centuries. A local brewery had operated in Moulin for several hundred years until it was closed in the early nineteenth century. To mark the hotel's 300th anniversary in 1995 the present hotelier, Chris Tomlinson, re-established the brewery in the old stables behind the hotel and it has since become a popular local attraction.

Moulin, Pitlochry

JV 23496

A charming view of the centre of Moulin in Victorian times with the village pump prominent in the foreground - piped water was still a long way into the future! The road from Pitlochry runs into the picture from the right and joins the old Great North Road by the hotel; it then bends to the left and becomes the village street. The addition of another wing to the hotel has meant that the end cottage of the row of houses visible to its left has been demolished but the remainder of the row is still standing. The church stands behind the trees on the left of the picture. Moulin is an ancient ecclesiastical centre which was founded by St Colman (or Colm) who came to Scotland with St Fillan around AD 490. The first known church in the village was built in 1613 and was enlarged in 1704 and again in 1787. This church had small windows and was very dark inside. Having been rebuilt yet again in 1834, it was gutted by fire in 1873 and rebuilt as the present church in 1875. The building was closed for worship in 1989 and sold in 2005. Its new owners are endeavouring to create a Centre of Historical Interest based on the history of the Parish of Moulin in particular and of Highland Perthshire in general. The old bell, which was cast in Rotterdam in 1749 by Peter Bakker and which survived the fire, is now displayed outside the church.

The old Scots word 'Gutcher' means 'Grandfather'. This gravestone, known as the 'Gutcher Stone', used to stand in Moulin churchyard, but in recent years it has been moved inside the church for its safety

The 'Queen's View' at the east end of Loch Tummel was one of Queen Victoria's favourite picnic locations, but it received its name long before she first visited it in 1866. No-one can be certain as to which queen it really is named after, but the two most favoured suggestions are that it was either named after the fourteenth-century Queen Isabella who was married to Robert the Bruce or after Mary, Queen of Scots, who held a great hunting party in the vicinity. Both suggestions are suspect, however, because it was not until Victorian times that people began to regard such scenery as beautiful rather than barbaric. A mystery indeed! Nowadays, the loch is much higher and wider because of the hydro-electric scheme that culminates a few miles downstream in the man-made Loch Faskally. Its present level is around 17 feet higher than in the picture.

Kynachan Lodge at Tummel Bridge was built in the early nineteenth century for Colonel David Stewart of Garth. Although once a private house, it is now the staff quarters for the nearby Tummel Hotel, which is owned by Lochs and Glens Holidays and which, although a modern hotel, has been built in sympathy with its beautiful surroundings.

The Dunfallandy Stone used to stand at the old chapel at Killiecrankie but was moved in the late nineteenth century to its present location on the west side of the Tummel near the mausoleum outside Dunfallandy House. The stone is an upright 5-inch-thick red sandstone slab, 5 feet high by approximately 2 feet 2 inches wide. Probably carved around the ninth century, it is sculptured in relief on both faces and displays beautifully carved patterns of the Celtic period. It is a Christian cross but its meanings are unknown. Nowadays it is enclosed in a glass case for its protection.

One of the most interesting tombstones in the old churchyard at Moulin is this one which is thought to commemorate a twelfth-century Crusader who was possibly a lord of the neighbouring Black Castle of Moulin. The stone shows a two handed sword, which measures 36 inches to the guard and 43 inches in total length. Now very worn, the stone also bears the inscription, 'WMD 1808 Aged 73' which shows this gravestone must have been reused in the nineteenth century.

The ruins of the Black Castle of Moulin stand about 350 yards south of the church. It was built around 1326 by Sir John Campbell of Lochow who was a son of Robert the Bruce's sister and was created Earl of Atholl by his cousin, David II. He was killed at the battle of Hallidon Hill in 1333. In 1500 the Black Death plague devastated the Highlands and many people died in the Moulin area. It is said that when the plague also broke out amongst the garrison at the castle, all the soldiers died from it and the castle was subsequently battered down by cannon to make a grave over them. The castle was originally surrounded by a moat but this was drained in 1720 to provide agricultural land.

The Dunalastair area (oddly, the name means 'Mount Alexander') near Kinloch Rannoch is the ancestral home of the Struan Robertsons. The original Dunalastair House was smaller and stood behind the one pictured here. In the mid-nineteenth century General Sir John MacDonald of Kinloch Rannoch purchased the property from a Robertson chief and built this magnificent baronial-style mansion on the left bank of the Tummel. He had the MacDonald arms cut high on the wall in the front of the house but, when the MacDonalds sold the house, the new proprietor who was Mr Tennent of Glasgow's Wellpark Brewery wanted the MacDonald coat of arms cut out of the wall. The gardener thought this might damage the building and suggested that a fast-growing creeper be planted which would soon cover it. This was agreed to; today the creeper has gone but the MacDonald coat of arms remains.

After Mr Tennant's death in 1891 the estate was sold to Mr J.C. Bunten, chairman of the Caledonian Railway, who had the mansion fitted with electric lighting. The estate subsequently came into the hands of the de Sales la Terriere family but when Mrs Jeannie de Sales la Terriere died in 1952 her son, Major James de Sales la Terriere, who lived nearby at Lochgarry, decided to sell the contents and abandon the house. By the early 1960s the house was officially classed as 'uninhabitable' and in the 1970s as 'ruinous' - it is still in that forlorn condition today.

Kinloch Rannoch lies on the River Tummel at the eastern end of Loch Rannoch. After the 1745 rebellion government Redcoats built roads from Tummel Bridge and around the side of Schiehallion, bridging the Tummel at the settlement here. At first the village was to have been populated by retired soldiers who would have been available to guard against further rebellions, but retired soldiers proved unsuited to the slow pace of Highland crofting life and so local inhabitants were given leases to their very own few acres of land. The *Ordnance Gazetteer of Scotland*, published around 1900, describes the village as 'a picturesque and thriving little place with a post office, money order facilities, savings bank and telegraph departments, two commodious hotels, a parish church (1829, renovated and improved in 1893), a Free Church (1855) and an Episcopal church, All Saints (1864 with 120 sittings).' The modern village centre is little changed from the picture except that the square is now paved. It still possesses two hotels, the parish church and the Episcopal church but the former Free church is now the village hall, the post office offers the Post Taste café, craft shop, tourist information and Internet facilities, whilst thrifty residents now have to await a twice-weekly visit from the Bank of Scotland mobile bank. The 21 feet high granite obelisk in the centre of the village was erected in 1875 to the memory of Dugald Buchanan, evangelist and sacred poet who, for the last 16 years of his life, was schoolmaster here. The public school, which had accommodation for 80 pupils, has been superseded by a modern junior school and its building is now the Kinloch Rannoch Outdoor Centre which is run by Perth & Kinross Council.

This photograph was taken from the road which runs from Rannoch Station along the north shore of Loch Rannoch into the village of Kinloch Rannoch at its eastern end. The trees and stone walls on the left hand side of the road have been replaced by hedges but the three terraced cottages with porches are still there. The middle one is now named 'Drumorveny' and the further one is 'Rose Cottage', whilst two new detached houses occupy the space taken up by the trees and stone wall on the right. The building with bow windows on the left at the very end of the avenue, and which fronts onto the village square, is the Dunalastair Hotel. This was built as an inn soon after the Battle of Culloden by returning government Redcoats and remained as such for well over 100 years until its development into a hotel in 1881 under the guiding hand of Major General Alastair Macdonald, whose title was 'Commander of the Forces'.

The mountain of Schiehallion rises 3,547 feet to the south east of Kinloch Rannoch and is the focal point in the panorama from the Queen's View at Loch Tummel. It was on its slopes in 1773 than an attempt was made by the Astronomer Royal, Nevil Maskelyne, to measure the mass of the earth using the displacement of a pendulum. Schiehallion was chosen for this purpose because of its isolation and its conical shape. Among those helping him was Charles Mason, who not only invented the contour line used in modern cartography but also gave his name to the 'Mason-Dixon' line which he had jointly surveyed with Jeremiah Dixon in 1763-67 and which in time came to broadly delineate the boundary between the free northern states and the slave-owning southern states of America. The bridge over the Tummel has the inscription 'This building erected A.D.1764 at the sole expense of His Majesty out of the Annexed Estates'. This was obviously intended to show King George III's personal generosity and improved stewardship of the estates forfeited after the 1745 rebellion. Traditionally, the route across the central Highlands continued along tracks across Rannoch Moor and through Glen Coe to Lochaber and beyond; this was the traditional 'Road to the Isles'.

This lonely church at Bridge of Gaur in the Braes of Rannoch on the South Loch Road was designed and built in 1907 by Peter MacGregor Chalmers. It has a plain harled exterior with round-arched Norman windows; it is likely that its birdcage bellcote, and possibly also its apse, were reused from earlier churches built in 1776 and 1855 on the same site. At one time it was intended that a road should be built across Rannoch Moor to Glencoe, thus making Kinloch Rannoch the central hub of the Highlands. Redcoats did indeed build a few miles of road westwards from their barracks at the head of the loch, but were unable to drain the desolate Rannoch Moor and the project was abandoned.

RANNOCH LODGE.

Rannoch Lodge was built in the eighteenth century and was formerly the seat of the Menzies family. By the mid-nineteenth century it had become the retreat favoured by some of the world's most prominent people. Andrew Carnegie, who became the richest man in the world, came here for three months in 1892 to escape serious industrial unrest at his Pittsburgh steel mills. In 1901, the year before his death, Cecil Rhodes worked here for a month on the final draft of his will to establish his scheme for Rhodes Scholars to study at Oxford. The young Winston Churchill was another house guest and Elizabeth Taylor was a frequent visitor in the 1970s and early 1980s. The building was almost destroyed by fire in the 1980s but has undergone restoration by its present owners. Four cottages on the estate are nowadays used as holiday cottages, namely the Gate Lodge, the Coach House, the Gamekeeper's House and the Ghillie's Cottage.

It was General Alistair MacDonald's ambition to operate a steamer service on Loch Rannoch and he had the S.S. *Gitana* brought to the loch in sections by horse and cart. This 90 feet long steamer was assembled on the shore and launched in 1881, but her powerful steam engine was not appreciated by other local landowners who refused to let him build a pier at Bridge of Gaur. He was forced to moor the steamer at the exposed east end of the loch where she sank during a storm in January 1882. The saloon windows were stove in, the vessel was swamped, and she lay 100 feet down at the bottom of the loch for almost a century. In 1982 she was salvaged but history repeated itself during her restoration. A similar violent storm arose in December 1983; she dragged her moorings and tragically was dashed to pieces on the shore.

Rannoch barracks was erected after the 1745 rebellion as a base for government troops. It is situated near to the point where the roads running along both sides of Loch Rannoch meet at Invercomrie. After the pacification of the Highlands was complete, Colonel Robertson of Struan, chief of Clan Donnochy, made his home at the barracks. The building is now a private house.

The scene in this photograph is the wild and desolate Gaur Valley at Dunan on Rannoch Moor, about half way between the west end of Loch Rannoch and Rannoch railway station. In this picture, which is obviously staged for the photographer because the vehicles are stationary, the couple in the pony and trap are probably heading to Rannoch Station to meet a friend or relation off the train. The public coach behind them, possibly the forerunner of today's postbus, may be carrying mails to be loaded onto the train or the driver may simply be hoping to pick up sporting passengers alighting from the train, wishing to be taken to their shooting lodge or to Kinloch Rannoch which lies 17 miles to the east. On their left the River Gaur winds its way past the small hamlet of Dunan on its way down from Loch Eigheach to Loch Rannoch.